CARL JOHNSON

Secrets of a Survivalist

Hope for the Best, but Plan for the Worst

Contents

Survivalist versus Prepper

Survivalist versus Prepper

When it comes to readiness for anything that life throws at you, there are survivalists and there are preppers. These terms are often used interchangeably, but they are actually very different. Survivalists and preppers have a common goal for sure, but there are major differences in the overall sentiment and outcome of their behavior.

A Common Bond

There are many commonalities between survivalists and preppers. At their core, both have the similar ideal of being ready for a disaster. Both survivalists and preppers alike spend time and resources to prepare for impending disasters such as major weather events, war, and even statistically unlikely disasters.

Both of these types of people have a strong will to live and make preparations for themselves and their families not only to survive a potentially disastrous event, but also after the event. Many of the preparations will involve supplies to allow them to continue to live without aid for an extended period of time.

Different Strokes

The difference between survivalists and preppers comes down to how seriously they take themselves. Make no mistakes about it, both of these groups of people are quite serious about their preparations for the future safety and comfort of themselves and their families. The core difference is really how seriously they take it, and how extreme their plans and preparations are.

There are also differences in how both of these groups prepare for unforeseen events and disasters. For example, one group might stockpile huge amounts of non-perishable foods while the other will have a smaller stockpile and rely heavily on seeds to grow their own food.

Survivalist Manifesto

Survivalists differ from preppers in the way they make their preparations and their overall idea of surviving after an event.

Survivalists, for example, tend to look to the Earth and wilderness for much of their survival needs. A survivalist will learn about the area around them and look to live off the land rather than having huge stockpiles. These people will likely hunt, forage, and grow their own food for their survival needs.

A survivalist is really exactly what their name suggests. They will do what needs to be done to survive. They do not expect to rely on the comforts of civilized life to sustain them during or in the aftermath of a disastrous event.

Prepper's Platform

Preppers differ from survivalists in how they plan to survive and even thrive after a disaster.

Preppers will usually have large stockpiles of supplies, non-perishable foods, and other items that will help them remain safe, alive, and even comfortable during and after such an event. A prepper will typically have a stockpile large enough not only to get them through the event, but large enough to sustain them until rescue.

Preppers are usually considered to be the more serious or fervent in their preparations. This might be because their preparations are often more visible to the people around them. The lengths at which preppers will prepare and stockpile are extremely varied from person to person.

Survivalists and preppers are different in the way they make their preparations and their overall ideals for how to survive, but at their core they are very similar. Both groups do the work and planning necessary to ensurethey not only survive a potential disaster, but thrive in the aftermath. They are both built on the platform of hard work, planning, and optimism that they will survive no matter what happens.

Survival Training

With all of the reality shows on television dedicated to survival techniques and even doomsday type preppers, you are likely somewhat familiar with the idea of survival training. But, what those television shows might not explain properly is that survival training isn't just for adventure buffs and the slightly paranoid.

Survival training is a very real and useful life tool that everyone should look into at some level. The fact is that being prepared for unforeseen disasters (such as destructive weather events, major industrial accidents, or even terrorism) is a responsible move.

What Is Survival Training?

Survival training is exactly what it sounds like. It is training you to survive outside of your usual comfort zone. Survival training can be taught for wilderness survival, or even urban survival should you ever be in a situation where you need to survive on your own in a city environment. There are many facets of survival training.

What Skills Are Taught?

Since there are so many types of survival training, the skill sets will vary, but most of the common core necessities will always be taught. These skills will revolve around food, water, shelter, and first aid.

Who Needs Survival Training?

Everyone needs to have at least a basic working knowledge of how to survive in many types of situations. Anyone could ever get lost in the woods, find themselves stranded anywhere, or find themselves in a disaster situation could seriously benefit from survival training.

Why Is Survival Training Necessary?

Catastrophic disasters are not all that far-fetched, and people get stranded or lost almost every day. If your car stalls on a deserted road with no way to call for help, you need to know what to do and how to proceed.

When Is a Good Time to Look into Survival Training?

There is never a bad time to look into survival training. Considering the fact that accidents and disasters of all types happen nearly every day, the sooner you are prepared for anything the better.

Will I Ever Really Use Survival Training?

Consider the old adage Hope for the best, but plan for the worst. Hopefully you will never have to use the skills you learn through survival training, but it certainly will help if you ever do.

Disasters Change Lives Forever

In the year 2005, natural disasters killed over 25,000 people and caused $57.7 billion in damage worldwide. Besides the obvious, direct impact of natural disasters (such as a tornado destroying a house), there are usually many indirect effects.

Although these effects may be less obvious, they are often times and can add years on to the recovery time from a disaster. As people who live in communities that have been devastated by a natural hazard will often say, there is no such thing as a complete recovery, disasters change lives forever.

Disaster Mitigation is the first link in the chain of disaster survival. Mitigation is the process of reducing the severity of the impact of natural hazards through planning. Each hazard requires a specific type of mitigation. In some cases, we can use engineering solutions.

Earthquake-resistant construction and devices to hold objects in place such as earthquake straps could at least reduce the impact of a natural hazard. In other cases, the only form of mitigation guaranteed to be successful is to limit or not allow human activities where the hazard occurs, such as floodplains, volcanoes and high fire risk areas.

But unfortunately, in some cases such as Hurricane Katrina and the Asian Tsunami, the fact that there was little or no planning or mitigation took its toll on human life. These types of disasters have a profound impact on us all. Prediction of natural disasters has improved greatly but more work needs to be done. Protection against disasters must continue in a logical, controlled and decisive manner.

The second link in the chain of disaster survival is personal preparation. Making plans for evacuation, having the correct survival supplies such as water and food that has a five-year shelf life, a flashlight that doesn't need batteries and a radio to stay connected to the outside world, is essential to us all. It is suggested that each person have at least 72 hours of supplies.

Statistically, the citizens of the United States are not prepared. Less 40% of the population has a plan and even less have supplies. The list of items is overwhelming to some people and just knowing where to start can be a conundrum.

Disasters do come in all forms and change our lives. We have seen it first hand in recent years. Mitigation, preparation and prediction will decrease loss of life and property. Every one of us must participate in disaster preparation. Some people say expect the unexpected but in reality we must anticipate the expected and prepare.

Are You Prepared For A Natural Disaster?

With the various types of natural disasters that have taken place in recent years, many people have started to realize they may not be prepared for such events to take place. While no one wants to think it can happen to them, we have all seen the footage of Hurricane Katrina and it was a reality that this type of natural disaster is something that does happen to real people. Even the fires spreading out of control in California remind us of the types of natural disasters that can take place.

It is important to pay close attention to the warnings that hopefully will be broadcast on TV and the if a natural disaster is possible. It is unbelievable the number of people ignore this information. If you are asked to evacuate the area do so as quickly and calmly as you can. Rescue efforts may not be available for those remain behind. It is a good idea to have a battery powered radio you can carry with you to continue listening to the instructions as you are traveling.

You should have an emergency supply kit on hand at all times just in case you do happen to be in a location where a natural disaster happens. Bottled water and canned foods can be stored for long periods of time. You want enough for each family member for at least five days.

Should you have to remain on your own for a few days until rescue teams can reach you these items will help you to survive. The food in your refrigerator can spoil if the power goes which is common after a natural disaster. Make sure you keep medications on hand for those need them on a regular basis.

If you have small children in the home make sure you have the necessary supplies on hand for them. Stocking up on personal items such as diapers, toilet paper, and toothpaste can help you to stay healthy during a natural disaster. Since you may be without power for several days you will want to have lanterns and flashlights readily available.

A small first aid kit with essential items can be useful because you never know when someone will be injured as a result of a natural disaster. Do your best to clean the injury and prevent infection until proper medical care can be received for the individual. Many people worry about their pets during a natural disaster but you may not be able to keep them with you during that time. If possible though store food for them as well so you won't be sharing the food you stored for your family with them.

A natural disaster can be very scary for everyone, but especially for children. Make sure that everyone is able to get plenty of rest and that children are allowed to openly share their feelings. Too many parents think it is best not to tell them what is going on but that tends to make them more afraid as they definitely know something is taking place around them.

After Disaster Sanitation Tips

In the aftermath of a disaster, staying clean might be one of the last thoughts on your mind. After all, who thinks of wet wipes when they are busy staying alive? Once the immediate danger has passed, however, sanitation is absolutely important and should be one of your priorities.

Hygiene Is Important

Keeping proper hygiene and sanitation can help prevent infection and illness. So it is very important to stay as clean as possible, and follow proper hygiene practices whenever you are able to. Hand washing especially is one of our strongest tools to fight the spread of germs and disease. Especially if you have any cuts or injuries, keeping those clean is of the utmost importance.

After an emergency, there may be special guidelines to follow to ensure safe and proper sanitation.

Listen to the Authorities

Especially after a flood type disaster, tap water might not be safe to drink or even bathe in. Follow the directions of your local authorities and wait for the go-ahead to use water from faucets.

Find Safe Water

When you are planning for emergency preparedness, stockpiling safe drinking water should be one of your biggest priorities. Not only does it ensure that you have enough water to drink, but there should be enough to brush teeth, wash hands, and follow other sanitation procedures.

Along with your drinking water, it is a good idea to keep a good amount of distilled water for cleaning wounds and washing hands.

Making Water Safe

When there are no other options besides the water around you or in the tap, you might have to doctor the water so that it is safe to use. This typically involves filtering, boiling or disinfecting the water that you have available to you.

Boiling: Filter the water as best as you can using towels or even coffee filters. If you do not have a filter, let the water stand for a while so that the sediment separates and settles, and then pour the clear water off the top. Bring the clear water to a full boil and let boil for at least one whole minute. Let the water cool and keep any water that isn't immediately used in clean, airtight containers.

Disinfecting: You can use iodine, water purification tablets, or even household (unscented) bleach to disinfect water. You will need to filter the water the same way, and then for the tablets or iodine follow directions from the manufacturer. For the bleach method, add 1/8 teaspoon of bleach per gallon of water, stir, and let sit for 30 minutes before use.

Last-Ditch Efforts

If you are not in a position to boil or disinfect your water, you can find water that is safe enough from many sources. In your home, the reserve water in your water heater tank and the water in your toilet tank (not the bowl) is usually safe to use as long as it hasn't been treated with cleaning chemicals. Outside the home, rainwater and water from moving bodies of water will be much cleaner and safer than standing water that could be infected.

Other Sanitation Options

Wet wipes, antibacterial gels, and sprays are not the most efficient at getting you clean when you are truly unsanitary (like after a disaster), but they will work if you have nothing else at your disposal.

After a disaster, the most important thing to have to stay sanitary and safe from germs and disease is clean water. Follow these tips and techniques to find or make clean water to keep healthy.

The Importance of Training the Mind for Survival

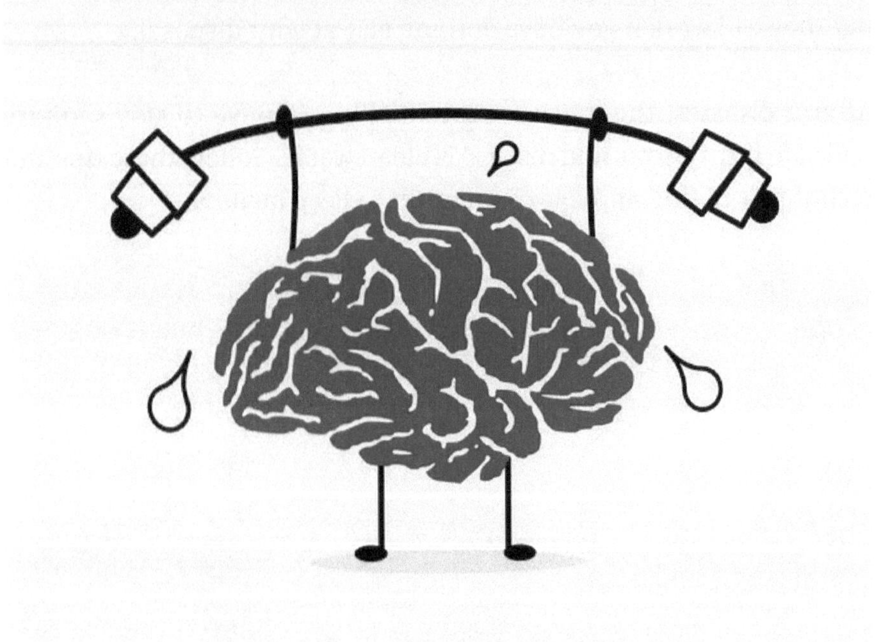

Sometimes as humans we don't fully understand the importance of the mind. In order to become a top survivalist you must first mentally prepare yourself. A mental survival kit is just as important as a physical survival kit. Training the mind for survival is very important to learning the secrets of a survivalist. Below you will find 6 important keys most survivalist have in common.

1. Willingness to learn. Even those who know nothing about survival until lost in the wilderness can still learn as they go - if they are willing to. If you're cold, watch that squirrel dive under a pile of leaves, and try that to stay warm (it works). Notice what's working and what isn't, and keep trying new things.

2. Willingness to do what's necessary. This is one of the most important items in your mental survival kit. Hey, they can eat hissing cockroaches just for the chance to win some money on "Fear Factor," so you can do it to save your life, right? Spoon with your buddy to stay warm, break open logs to find grubs to eat - do whatever it takes.

3. Positive attitude. This is an essential. In many stories of survival it is clear that those who expected to survive did. Even if you're not sure you can survive, encourage this attitude by acting as if you expect to.

4. Inspirational thoughts. This is how to have that positive attitude. An easy and enjoyable way to get this inspiration is to read true stories of wilderness survival. Some of the stories are about situations far worse than anything you are ever likely to encounter. Remembering them at the appropriate time is a sure way to see that you can survive. them to others too, if you are in a group.

5. Wilderness survival knowledge. You don't have to go to a survival training school to read and remember you can safely eat all North American mammals, or that you can stuff your jacket with cattail fluff to create a winter coat. Any little bit helps, so learn a new trick or two each season, or take an edible plant guide on your next hike.

6. Reasons to survive. We all have reasons to want to live, but we need to remember to pull out those reasons when the time comes. Many people have attributed their survival to the constant thought of a loved one waiting for them, or something they want in the future.

Maybe you've already done this mental preparation, but it can't hurt to look over the list above again. Is there anything you need to work on in your mental survival kit?

What Every Survival Kit Should Contain

Every home and car should contain at least a basic survival kit in the event of a disaster. Even if you believe that nothing will ever happen to necessitate using such a kit, it is always better to be safe than sorry when it comes to the lives and safety of yourself and your loved ones. You just never know what the future could bring, and a survival kit for emergency preparedness is essential to any home.

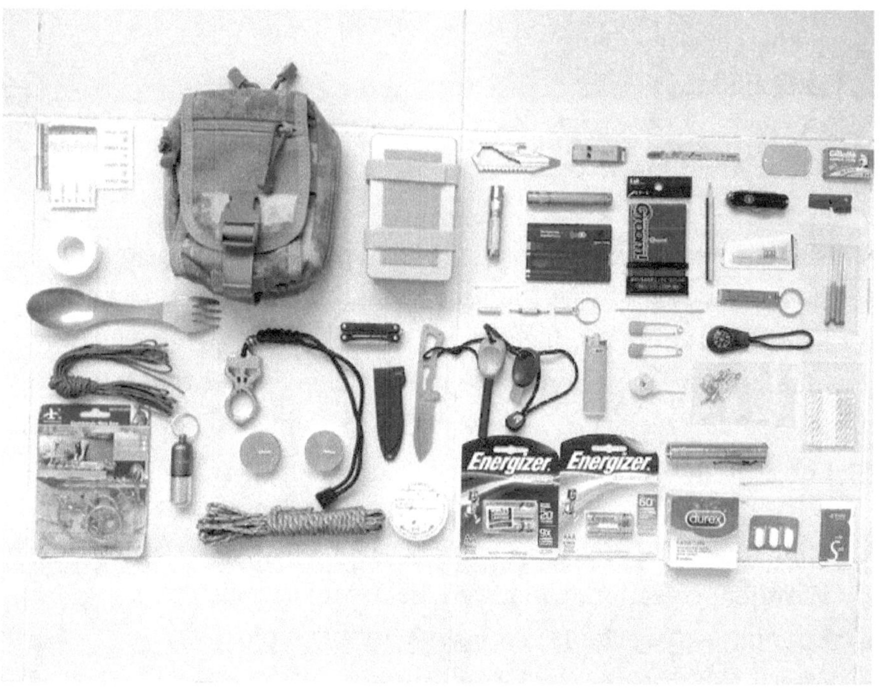

The Very Basics

At the very least, every home should have a few basics. These items will be especially helpful in the event of a power outage of any sort, especially if you are unable to leave your home due to weather or safety reasons.

* Bottled water (at least one gallon per person per day)
   * Non-perishable food items
   * Extra clothing, blankets, etc.
   * LED flashlights
   * Plenty of batteries
   * Waterproof matches or lighter
   * Health and sanitation supplies (toilet paper, soap, hygiene products)
   * Documentation (identification, medical history and medication lists, emergency contacts)
   * First aid kit

Ready for Anything

A disaster in your own home opens you up to a lot of possibilities for survival. There are always tools, supplies, and items that can be used for a multitude of tasks. If a disaster strikes and for whatever reason you need to leave your home, you want to be ready for that too. These items should be ready to pick up and go at a moment's notice, and note that these items are in addition to the basic items already covered.

* A multi-use tool (such as a Leatherman or Swiss army knife)
   * Weather protection: sunscreen, hats, rain jackets, etc.
   * Communication items (such as a portable radio)
   * Map
   * A plan

Planning Ahead

Having a plan is one of the strongest tools in your arsenal. Knowing where to go or what to do in an emergency situation is perhaps more useful than almost any item in your survival kit. Planning ahead includes having your survival kit at the ready, having a primary and secondary plan for where to go if you have to leave your home, knowing basic first aid and how to read a map or use a shortwave radio, and other general basic knowledge. A plan exponentially increases the odds that you could survive just about anything that comes along.

The Importance of First Aid

Having a survival first aid kit is another super important key factor that absolutely should not be overlooked.

Red Cross first aid kit list:

* 2 absorbent compress dressings (5 x 9 inches)
   * 25 adhesive bandages (assorted sizes)
   * 1 adhesive cloth tape (10 yards x 1 inch)
   * 5 antibiotic ointment packets (approximately 1 gram)
   * 5 antiseptic wipe packets
   * 2 packets of aspirin (81 mg each)
   * 1 blanket (space blanket)
   * 1 breathing barrier (with one-way valve)
   * 1 instant cold compress
   * 2 pair of non-latex gloves (size: large)
   * 2 hydrocortisone ointment packets (approximately 1 gram each)
   * Scissors
   * 1 roller bandage (3 inches wide)
   * 1 roller bandage (4 inches wide)
   * 5 sterile gauze pads (3 x 3 inches)

* 5 sterile gauze pads (4 x 4 inches)
* Oral thermometer (non-mercury/non-glass)
* 2 triangular bandages
* Tweezers
* First aid instruction booklet

Other Items to Consider

Depending on your family and specific needs, you may want to consider a few more items to add to your kit. Remember that the idea is emergency preparedness, so try to think of everything. For example, if someone in your family has anaphylactic allergies, you will want to consider adding an EpiPen and/or Benadryl to your survival first aid kit.

Some other items to consider include:

* LED flashlight
    * Extra batteries
    * Burn gel
    * Medical grade super glue (cyanoacrylate base)
    * Suture kit
    * Eye wash kit
    * Necessary medications for family members

You will also want to keep information about each of your family members' medical history and a list of medications that each of you take. When rescue services do come, it could help them to have a working knowledge of your history in the event of an injury or emergency. Also keep a list of contacts and emergency phone numbers so you can reach family or friends if you need help or to tell them you are okay.

Other Survival Kit Options

There are online forums and websites that specialize in emergency preparedness and disaster readiness. Some of these sites even sell survival kits, but they are often quite expensive. To save money and be able to cater the kit to the personal needs of you and your family, take a little time and put together your own survival kit, starting with these minimum necessary items.

Why Plan for Something That May Never Happen?

Preparing for a disaster is a necessary part of living a responsible life. You want to hope that such an event never occurs, but be prepared for anything to keep your family safe. If you don't have one already, start building your survival kit today.

Emergency Preparedness: How to Budget for What You Need

In an emergency situation, you want to have a number of supplies you can fall back on to ensure your survival, health, and safety. This requires collecting and maintaining a decent amount of those supplies even though you may never need them. Altogether, these supplies – including food and water stockpiles, first aid supplies, and even the most basic survival kits, can add up.

Do Your Research

If you are starting from scratch, do some research on emergency preparedness. Look to websites such as The American Red Cross and CDC Emergency Preparedness for lists and ideas of what you need to build a survival kit and items to stockpile for emergencies. You can also search your local area for survivor training and tips.

Once you have ideas of certain items you need, research those too. Some items, like food and water, are pretty foolproof. However, other items such as shelter building supplies, weather clothing and gear, and first aid supplies, are not created equal. Knowing what to look for can save you money while also guaranteeing you have the best products on hand.

Make a List

Before you go out and buy everything you need, make a detailed list of what items you need for your emergency preparedness or survival kit. Break the list up into sections based on their categories such as sustenance, shelter, first aid, and more.

Also have an idea of how much everything on that list costs as well. For home stockpiles, most experts recommend that you have a minimum of three days' worth of supplies, but at least two weeks' worth is preferred.

Build Up to It

Especially if you are starting from scratch, buying all of the items you need at once might not be very budget friendly. You might have to get one or two items at a time, and build up to the full amount of items needed.

Prioritize

To know what items to purchase first, prioritize the list you made based on items that are the most important and most useful. The top three items to prioritize are:

* Water: Having enough water stockpiled is one of the most important survival tips. Keep bottled water both in your car and your home. For your home stockpile, the best rule of thumb is to have one gallon of water per person per day.

* First aid: A good emergency first aid kit and basic first aid knowledge is another item to prioritize. The American Red Cross has a detailed list of items that should be in any first aid kit. You will need to add or make changes to that list based on your family size and specific medical needs.

* Food: The most likely disaster situation involves a severe weather event where you could be stuck in your home for days or more without

electricity or water. Having a decent stockpile of non-perishable foods to keep you and your family nourished is very important.

Keep an Eye Out

As you are building up your emergency preparedness supplies, keep an eye out for good deals, coupons, and sales.

Maintenance

Some basic maintenance will help save you money and keep your survival supplies up to date. Keep your food and water stores rotating as they come near their expiration dates. That way things can be used rather than thrown out and stores kept fresh in case of emergency. Proper maintenance of any tools and other equipment will keep them from needing to be replaced, which will also save you money.

Emergency preparedness is a responsible and potentially life-saving life skill, but being ready for anything isn't always cheap. You can ensure the safety of your family and your budget with these tips.

Emergency Preparedness: Tools to Help You Stay Organized

In virtually any situation, staying organized can make things much easier. Having an organized emergency preparedness plan and supplies could literally save your life should disaster ever strike.

Here are some tips and tools to help you organize your emergency preparations.

Write Out Your Plan

First of all, you want to organize your thoughts. The best way to do this is to write out your emergency plan. Not only will it help you think it through, but it will also help you crack down on details and get everyone involved on the same page.

Don't forget to include different scenarios in your plans for emergencies. Make a plan for every situation you can think of: fires, floods, tornadoes, power outages, nearby industrial accidents, and whatever else comes to mind - including anything which is more likely to happen because of the climate in your area (such as snowstorms).

Set That Plan into Motion

Once you have a plan, you can set your plan into motion by making preparations as needed. For example, get all of your survival equipment ready including emergency items in the house, in the car, etc.

Lists for Everything

To keep track of what you have done, what needs to be done, and what or where everything is, never underestimate the usefulness of a detailed list.

Inventory: Keep a running inventory list for your emergency food and water rations, first aid kit, and other supplies. Include expiration dates and make changes to the list as items are used, removed, or replaced.

Emergency information: Remember to keep a list of medical information, medications, emergency contacts, and any other useful information. Not only will lists like this help you keep everything straight in the chaotic aftermath of a major event, but it will also help emergency services should you be unable to talk.

Specialize a Space

In your car, office, home, and wherever else you might be during a crisis, specialize a space for your emergency supplies. Have a bag in your car or office, and designate a pantry, shelf, or other area at home for emergency water and food rations and other supplies.

Contain It

Especially when storing food, make sure that all items are safely and hygienically contained in airtight bags or containers. Have extra containers on standby for any cans, boxes, or bags that are opened for use. Keep everything as neatly contained as possible so you can keep track of and locate items you need.

Label It

Label all of your supplies clearly. When an emergency occurs, you might not have the time or frame of mind to dig through a mess to look for small items. Also label items with expiration dates and date opened so that you can avoid waste and keep supplies fresh.

Maintain It

Save time, money, and trouble by maintaining all of your hard-earned organization. Keep everything as clean as possible, and rotate supplies so nothing is expired when you need it most.

A little organization can go a long way, especially in an emergency situation. You can boost your preparations by following these tips and ideas for organizing your emergency plans and supplies.

Safe Drinking Water in an Emergency or Disaster

Nothing makes clearer the importance of water than a large disaster; clean, fresh water becomes more valuable than gold. It's easy to forget that without water, we just can't survive. 60 percent of our bodies are water, in fact for infants, water makes up about 80 percent of their body, so it is even more vital they have access to clean drinking water.

Unfortunately, following large-scale disasters, it's not unusual that water supplies may be cut off temporarily or be rendered unfit for consumption. Everyone should know the following tips about safe drinking water in emergency situations.

Preparedness is Everything: The advice comes over and over, but most people still are not ready when disaster hits. You must maintain a supply of clean drinking water someplace safe in your home. You can survive a week without food, if necessary, but even one or two days without water can be fatal.

In terms of how much water is needed to be stored, you need to drink at least two quarts a day of water. Enough water for all the members of your family for at least a few days is a good idea. You can store water yourself in your own containers; anything glass, and clean, thoroughly washed plastic containers with caps work well. Seal water tightly in their containers and store them in someplace cool and dark in your home. Make sure to change new water regularly; once every six months.

Finding Safe Drinking Water: If you do run out of water during an emergency, or are trapped somewhere without ready access to clean drinking water, you'll need to know what's safe to drink, and what isn't.

After a disaster, possible sources of safe drinking water in your home include the water from your hot water tank, the water from your toilet tank (not the bowl, but the water from your tank, but if it is chemical-free), and water trapped in your water pipes. Melt any ice cubes that you may have stored.

Avoid using water from waterbeds as drinking water, since they are treated with chemicals unsafe for drinking. You can use waterbed water for washing, though. Outside your home try to locate streams, rivers, lakes, or other sources of fresh water. Never drink floodwater; it is usually contaminated with bacteria and chemicals. Do save rainwater that may fall for drinking.

Purifying Water in an Emergency: If you cannot locate safe drinking water during an emergency, then any water you find that does not look clear, or which you believe may be contaminated, should be purified before drinking.

The best and easiest way to purify water is by boiling. Disease-bearing microorganisms cannot survive in high temperatures. Boil the water for about one minute. For improved taste, pour the water back and forth from one clean container to another.

If you're unable to boil your water, treat it chemically before drinking. Household chlorine bleach can be used to treat your water. Use an eyedropper, to drop eight drops of bleach into each gallon of water to be treated. Make sure the chlorine you use lists hypochlorite as its only active ingredient; any extra chemicals or fragrances will only further contaminate the water. Stir the water and allow it to stand at least 30 minutes. When the water appears clear, it is likely safe to drink. If it is still murky or clouded, put in eight more drops and let stand another 30 minutes.

How to Melt Ice and Snow to Find Drinking Water to Survive

Water is extremely important to survival. Since the body is comprised of about 75%of water, it is no doubt that we need water on a regular basis. Did you know that humans can survive for weeks without food, but only a few days without adequate water? Even in cold climates, water can be crucial to survival.

Everyone knows the importance of water during the heat of summer, but water is equally important in cold weather, as well. You lose water by sweating during strenuous activity. Breathing is another way you lose valuable fluids. Dehydration promotes chilling and risk of frostbite or hypothermia.

Finding a source for safe drinking water should be a priority for you if you should ever become stranded in the wilderness. Don't wait until the first signs of dehydration to set in before you start looking for water to drink. Finding water takes time and energy, so start early.

As in any survival situation, always look for surface water first. It is possible to find water in streams, lakes, and rivers, but more than likely, your supply of drinking water is bound to be in the frozen form of snow or ice, when in the cold months of winter or Arctic climates.

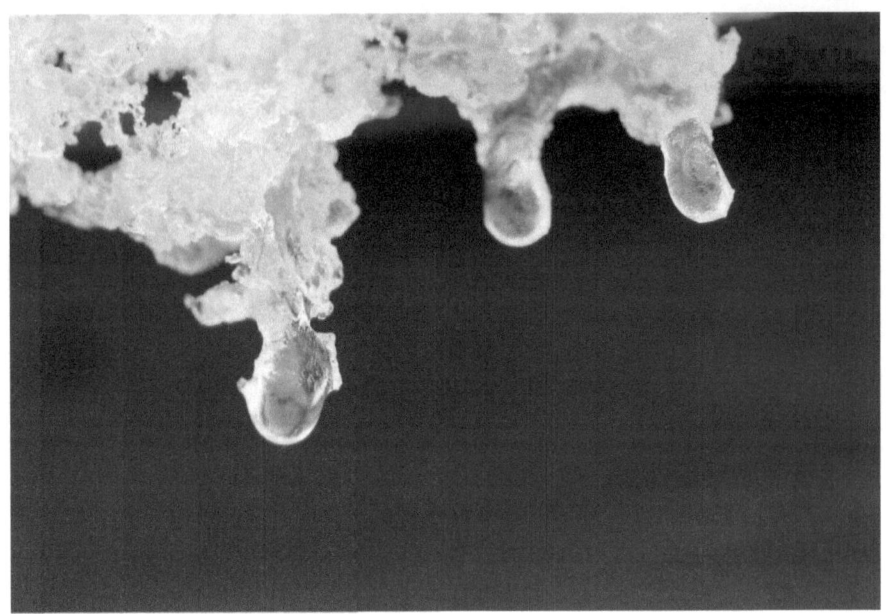

It may seem so obvious to just scoop up some snow and eat it like ice cream to replenish your lost fluids. This is not a good idea. Never place snow or ice in your mouth. Doing this can harm the inside of your mouth. Also, the cold temperature of the ice or snow will only make you colder.

To begin making water from ice or snow, gather clean snow or ice. If possible, use ice instead of snow. Ice provides more valuable water than snow. Also, ice melts faster than snow.

When melting snow or ice, be certain you have enough fuel wood. It takes a long time to melt snow or ice into drinking water.

Don't place a bunch of snow into your melting pot. The fire will not produce water in this way. It is best to begin by placing just a small portion of snow or ice in the pot. Once this melts, add just a bit more snow or ice to be melted into water. Add just enough until it floats freely in the water. Continue the process.

Another method to try is by using a piece of clothing as a sack for the snow. Tie the sleeves of a T-shirt and fill it with snow or ice. Suspend the sack over a container that is next to your fire. The water will filter through The shirt and into the container.

Water is essential for survival even in cold, winter climates. Gather drinking water by melting snow and ice slowly. Keeping yourself hydrated will allow the best chances of survival. Drinking enough water to replenish lost fluids can help to prevent frostbite and hypothermia. Remember, melting ice and snow takes a considerable amount of time, so plan ahead for your drinking needs in a winter climate survival situation.

How to Purify Water for Outdoor Survival in an Emergency

We are used to the luxury of walking over to the sink and having safe water at our fingertips fresh from the tap, but in the wild, water is not generally safe for drinking. Because water is seldom pure, it is essential to know how to purify water for outdoor survival in an emergency.

If you are not absolutely certain the water is safe, you must purify it. Clean water is crucial to good health and survival. Water that is polluted can contain microorganisms that can cause serious illness. Viruses and bacteria can really take a toll on someone out in the wilderness. Stomach issues are not pleasant in the comfort of home, let alone out in the wild. Do what you can to protect yourself.

Chemical pollutants are also a concern in some areas. Such chemicals are often herbicides or pesticides from farming industries. This form of is another problem that we cannot see in the water.

There are three main ways to purify water. Filtration is one method for cleaning water that removes the visible particles in the water. Your sock or T-shirt can become a filter or strainer to remove dirt and debris from the water. A filtering water bottle can be a useful tool for an outdoor survival kit. Do remember that filtering water is not the same as purifying water.

Boiling is a safe way to remove harmful microorganisms. Boiling water does not remove chemical pollutants from the water. Water must boil rapidly for just a few minutes to be safe, but in some cases, this method is not practical. If you are able to create a fire, you may be able to boil the water sufficiently for safety.

Many outdoor survival kits include iodine or purification tablets to purify water and make it safe for consumption. Check the contents of your outdoor survival kit to see if such items are included. If not, purchase this item to supplement your current outdoor survival kit. Learn how to use the specific products that you have available. Follow the directions carefully for any chemicals to purify your water. The water is safe to drink using such methods, but know that the taste does not improve.

To improve the taste of your drinking water, it is a good idea to combine and purification methods for the best taste.

A combination of these methods can make the water safe and improve the taste. It is crucial to locate water and make it healthy for consumption in an outdoor survival situation. Use what items you have with you, as well as, the items found in nature.

Begin with the water that appears the clearest. Moving surface water is always the first choice whenever available. Stagnant water is the least favorable for survival. Water that is not moving and shows no sign of life is a warning to you. Stay away from such water whenever possible.

Safe, pure water is key to survival. Dehydration is a real concern in an outdoor survival situation. Use purification methods to ensure your good health during outdoor survival situations. Staying hydrated with clean drinking water can allow you to survive for a significant period of time in the wilderness.

Finding Food for Outdoor Survival

Humans need water to sustain themselves, long before food becomes an absolute necessity, but if you have ever pondered a situation where you are alone in the wilderness, you probably first thought about food and shelter. Learning how to find food in the wild is a valuable outdoor survival skill.

We are so accustomed to the luxury and convenience of walking over to the fridge. And grabbing a snack or cruising through the drive-through of the local restaurant that finding food in the great outdoors seems frightening to many individuals.

In reality, nature often provides foods that are nourishing if you know where to look. Granted, these items may not taste as delectable and palatable as a cheeseburger or steak made-to-order, but they do provide necessary nourishment and energy to survive.

Plants are a form of nourishment if you know which ones are edible and safe. Learn about plants and their edible parts by reading up on the topic or taking a hike with an experienced guide. Be wary of any unknown plants that may cause a harmful reaction.

Do be aware that some parts of plants may be edible while other parts of the plant are not. Focus on studying specific plants that are abundant in your area of travel. Learn which plants are edible and what varieties are poisonous in your region.

Animals are another option for food when it comes to survival. Humans need protein to survive and nature often provides wild animals for this purpose. If you are alone in the wilderness, you can trap animals for food. Also, if surface water is available in the area, fishing is a great option.

If animal trapping and hunting isn't your specialty, it is important to learn about this outdoor survival skill before you actually need it. Fishing requires some technique, as well. Learn from watching survival shows, reading from books or the , or first-hand from someone experienced in the trade.

Preparation of the fish and game is equally as important as knowing how and where to find the animals. Learning the fish that are safe to eat, for example is an outdoor survival skill, but knowing how to prepare the fish is a completely different task at hand. Some fish are safe to eat raw, but others, must be cooked.

Insects and worms are other forms of nutrition in the wild. These animals are often abundant in most any environment. Learn what types of bugs are safe for eating. Worms and insects can provide valuable protein.

To survive, you will probably need to open your mind to new forms of food that are initially unappealing to you. Getting over the unappetizing idea is one of the largest issues for survivors, but it can be done in an emergency.

To be adequately prepared for an outdoor survival situation, you must learn the survival skills necessary to find food. Educate yourself about edible plants, wild game, and safe fish. Once you are knowledgeable about what you can eat, then it is important to learn how to prepare the food for consumption. This information can save your life in an emergency outdoor survival situation.

Drawbacks to Hunting Mammals for Survival

When it comes to our survival, we often think about what we will have to eat for food. Although water is much more important to our survival in the great outdoors, we often allow our minds to wander to edible meat when we think about pangs of hunger. Mammals can provide nourishment for humans stranded in the wild, but they may not be our best option for food in a survival situation.

Although Americans typically view mammals to be one of the tastiest foods in the wild, there are numerous drawbacks and disadvantages to hunting mammals for survival in an emergency.

Nearly all mammals will use their teeth to protect themselves if necessary. The size of the animal indicates the amount of danger it presents, but don't underestimate any animals. Even a squirrel can inflict a serious wound.

If an animal becomes cornered it will defend itself. If no escape route is available for the mammal, it may show aggression and become dangerous. Mothers, in particular, are capable of becoming extremely aggressive. They want to defend their young and will do nearly anything to protect them.

All mammals are considered edible. The bearded seal and polar bear have dangerous levels of vitamin A in their liver. Beware of the poisonous glands on the platypus. This mammal is native to Australia and Tasmania.

Large mammals such as caribou or elk may seem so tempting to the taste buds, but such animals are difficult to trap for food. Smaller mammals are often easier to trap or snare. Preparing small mammals is typically easier than larger animals. If you simply feel you must find a mammal for food to survive, the smaller animals are more abundant.

Another drawback is mammals will usually detect the traps set for them in the wilderness. This fact makes the inexperienced hunter less likely to find the nourishment they need to survive. Other forms of food may be available with less effort.

You will want to consider options that are abundant in your environ-
ment. Are there birds and fish in the area for you to eat? Maybe a healthy handful or two of ants could provide adequate protein and nourishment

without the danger. Open your mind to all options available to you.

Insects, for instance, don't sound as tasty as a deer, but they can provide 65 to 80% protein. This is remarkable when compared to the mere 20% of protein found in beef.

Despite what we would typically think of as preferable, meat is not always completely necessary for survival. Consider a vegetarian diet. Numerous edible plants are excellent sources of nutrition for the survivor.

Although mammals initially appear to be the option, there are numerous drawbacks to this choice of food for survival. Always keep your goal of survival in mind. Open your mind up to other cuisine if it is readily available and nourishing without the dangers associated with hunting mammals. Fish, insects, and edible plants are other ways to find nourishment for energy during an emergency.

How to Find a Natural Shelter for Survival

A shelter is crucial to your survival if you are stuck or stranded in the wilderness. Sometimes, you don't have the necessary tools and supplies, to build an adequate shelter, available to you. Look around, nature has probably given you something to work with if you stop for a moment to assess the situation.

Don't allow your mind to make the situation more difficult. Take a moment to stop and really look at your options. You will probably be pleasantly surprised at the numerous shelter options available to you.

Because the rain, sun, and extreme temperatures are hard on the body, you will need to find shelter quickly. Your current environment offers shelter to numerous species of animals. You, too, can also take shelter from the natural landscape.

A simple log, for instance, can be useful for protection. If the log is at the right angle to the wind, it becomes a handy windbreak for you to use for protection. Another fantastic idea is to use another log or stick to dig out a hollow area in the ground, where you can sit or lie down, to further protect yourself from the elements.

Hollow trees and logs are another option for shelter in a serious survival situation. Whether the tree is standing or has fallen down, it can provide some shelter. Broken boughs or sweeping branches can offer protection from the hot sun, pouring rain, or howling wind.

Overhangs and caves can provide a area to rest and relax. Use some rocks or debris and sticks to form a door to the shelter area for even greater protection from the elements. Caves can be home to animals such as insects, snakes, or other dangerous creatures, so be cautious when exploring these areas as a potential natural shelter.

Even in snowy weather, you can take shelter beneath a medium-sized tree. Pockets may form beneath the branches near the trunk. Dig in the snow to locate such areas to use for shelter. Stay inside an open pocket of snow. Cover yourself up with snow to use as insulation. Your body heat will remain in this area, rather than escaping, and help to keep you warm. This will reduce the risk of frostbite and hypothermia.

If you are in an area that is completely open, sit with your back to the wind. Pile any supplies or belongings behind you to act as a windbreak for protection.

You should always select your shelter area wisely. Your shelter must be safe for survival. Try to avoid dangerous areas with falling rocks or falling trees. Proper drainage and ventilation are also key to survival. Areas that are too close to water may be dangerous due to flooding.

You can use logs, hollows, or caves to protect yourself from the wind, sun, and weather. Even your supplies or broken limbs can offer some comfort. Finding a safe shelter to sleep and rest is crucial to your survival in an emergency. You can use the assets of the environment to protect yourself until help arrives.

Choosing the Right Survival Shelters

To create a successful and comprehensive emergency plan and survival kit, you have to think ahead and consider everything. There is more to a survival plan than extra water and batteries. You need to also consider what you need to have to survive outside of your home for a potentially extended amount of time.

Survival shelters are as varied as the people that build and live in them. Some shelters are so simple you can keep all of the supplies in a small bag; others are more complicated than huge, underground luxury homes. Whatever kind of survival shelter you use, there are some factors to consider.

How Many People

Planning a survival shelter for a family of three is a bit less complicated than a family of fifteen. While you, your spouse, and your child might be able to cozy up in a tent or under a tarp, it's pretty unlikely that your whole extended family could fit in there with you. This is something to keep in mind when choosing a survival shelter.

How Long Are You Planning For

How long you plan for is up to you. Most survival manuals and experts recommend planning for 72 hours to two weeks at the very least to allow time for rescue after a disastrous event. Some people prefer to build or purchase a survival shelter they could live in for an extended period of time. So this is something to think about as well, because a simple tent or tarp might only last you so long.

Portable or Built In

As mentioned before, survival shelters come in many forms. Would you prefer to be able to take your shelter on the road with you, or would you prefer it to be built underground where you will remain stationary?

Location

If you are planning to build a stationary shelter, deciding on the location matters as well. You might decide to build a shelter right on your home property, or you might choose a secluded area so you are hidden from any potential wanderers or other dangers.

Comforts of Life

What you want or need inside your survival shelter will help to determine the type or size of shelter best for you. Some people only want the very basics, with enough space for everyone to be inside safely with a small stockpile of supplies. Others prefer to go all out, with bedrooms, kitchens, and bathrooms.

Types of Survival Shelters

1. The most basic

Tarp: A relatively basic structure can be built with a tarp and some rope. It might not be fancy, but it will provide some cover from the wind and rain and can travel with you just about anywhere.

Tent: A decent tent will protect you quite a bit more than just a tarp, and can also be taken down and put back up easily, and carried with you if you find yourself on the move.

2. Intermediate options

Storm shelter: Storm shelters can be above ground or below ground, and can be installed just about anywhere on your property without being too expensive. Most of these shelters are going to be pretty basic, with a sitting room for a few people and a small area for supplies. These shelters are usually for short-term shelter, but could potentially sustain you for a few days if you have enough supplies.

Small bunker: Whether near your home or in a secret location, bunkers can be built underground and provide a few more comforts than a basic storm shelter. Some bunkers can be built with bathroom facilities and more than one room.

3. Home away from home

Some bunkers go all out, really providing you with a home away from home. These bunkers can range from small apartments, to large living facilities where quite a few people can live comfortably. These bunkers can even be built with all the amenities you are used to in your daily life, including plumbing, electricity, and even cable and hookups.

Choosing the right survival shelter for you depends on the factors listed as well as your own preferences. Sometimes decisions are made based on budget and timing. Do your research before deciding which survival shelter will be best for you, and remember to cover all of your bases so you are ready if an emergency strikes.

How to Make a Debris Hut Shelter for Survival in the Wilderness

A debris hut only takes an hour or two to make. Your debris hut will protect you by allowing you to sleep under leaves and sticks, for instance, while keeping the wind blocked. This will protect both you and your blanket of debris.

Shelter is extremely important when you are facing a survival situation. Since the body is not fully equipped to face the elements on its own, it is crucial you know how to protect yourself from the rain, snow, and sun. Extreme temperatures are harsh on the body, so the skill of creating a debris hut is valuable in an outdoor survival emergency.

To make a debris hut for shelter, begin with a fallen tree or pole that is about 1.5 to 2 times your height. This will become the center pole for your hut. Hold this main beam of the hut off the ground with a stump, forked tree, or rock. The item must be somewhat sturdy. It should be about as high as you when you are seated.

Plan now to make the door of your debris hut shelter away from the direction of the prevailing wind. This will help to protect you from the cold of the night by not allowing the cool wind to directly blow on you.

You can make a framework for your debris hut by placing large limbs against the main beam of the shelter. This should be done at angles of about 45 degrees. Your debris hut looks similar to a low tent or triangle.

Use smaller sticks and limbs to offer protection from the wind and rain by placing such items against the framework of the debris hut shelter. It is best to use dead grass, small sticks, fern, or leaves to make insulation for your debris hut shelter. This layer of insulation should be about 3 feet thick for adequate protection.

Cover the insulation of the hut with small light branches. This will keep the insulation in place. You do not want the wind blowing your shelter and protection away. In winter climates, piling snow on the insulation layer can help to further insulate the debris hut shelter from the wind and cold. Creating a shelter that can keep you warm and reasonably comfortable will allow you to sleep and rest and conserve precious energy.

Body heat can be lost very quickly by laying directly on the bare ground. Place debris on the floor of the debris hut shelter. Select items that would be comfortable for you to sleep on such as leaves or dead grass. Comfort may seem a luxury at this point in the battle for survival, but inadequate rest can leave you tired. Exhaustion leads a poor attitude and outlook which directly influences your chances of survival.

Keep extra insulation items and debris close to the opening to the shelter. This will allow you to drag it over to create a door for your hut.

A debris hut shelter is a simple way to use the items in the wilderness to protect yourself from the elements. Knowing how to properly make a shelter can help you to survive in serious situations.

What Type of Survival Clothing Should I Pack?

Putting together a survival kit in case of emergencies or disaster is part of being a responsible adult. To protect yourself and your family, put together a kit of emergency preparedness items that will get you through should a need ever arise. What you put in your kit is important, and there are many lists out there that outline the many different items that you should include. Survival clothing is one of the items almost always included on that list.

What Qualifies As Survival Clothing?

Unfortunately those lists don't always specify exactly what you need. So the words extra clothing or survival clothing might not come across as anything very special or important.

When you are stuck in your home or car without power during a snowstorm, survival clothing will have more meaning to you. And when you are walking miles and miles across a desert after being stranded due to car troubles, survival clothing will have more meaning to you. No matter what situation you may find yourself in, survival clothing is an important part of emergency preparedness.

Harsh Weather Months

Survival clothing is especially important during the harsh weather months when temperatures can soar or plummet, and the weather is doing nothing to help you stay safe. Depending on where you are, the temperatures alone could hurt you, not to mention rain, snow, and all sorts of inclement weather. The clothing that you are wearing, and the extra items you have with you, can make all the difference when it comes to saving your life.

Winter

In the winter, of course, your main goals are to stay warm and dry. Extra sweaters, coats, socks, and proper footwear like boots are all important items to keep on hand. Gloves, hats, and socks are small items that can save your life.

Summer

Summer is all about sun protection. Sunscreen, hats, scarves, and protective eyewear can all help keep you safe from the harsh rays of the sun.

Lightweight, light colored, long sleeved shirts that cover you up without overheating you are a good idea to keep as well. As much as you'll want to strip off every piece of clothing you have just to stay cool, your clothes help keep the sun off and moisture in.

Milder Weather Months

While the harsher weather months are certainly more dangerous, do not underestimate the dangers of the seemingly mild weather months. Spring and fall might offer more comfortable weather, but there are still extremes to fight.

Spring

No matter how mild it is, remember to protect yourself from the sun all year long. On top of your sun protective gear, you will want to have something warm with you as well. It might be too warm during the day, and then temperatures could plummet at night and during the early morning, so be ready for anything.

Fall

Just like spring, temperatures can be erratic during the fall. When you are out walking all day long without shelter, the sun can become dangerous. Conversely, temperatures can still fall below freezing so you have to be ready for whatever the weather throws at you.

All-Weather Items

No matter what season, there are some survival clothing items that should be kept at all times. Depending on where you are or your own preferences, you may need to add to this basic list:

* Gloves
    * Waterproof and sun blocking hat
    * Parka or rain jacket
    * Snow/rain boots

Putting together a survival kit is one step that you are taking to keep you and your family safe. Understanding why each item is needed can help you make good decisions about what goes into your survival kit. Survival clothing can vary from season to season, and according to the area you live in.

How to Make a Fire for Outdoor Survival

Survival in the wilderness can be tough. But know that it is possible. One of the first lessons to survival is learning how to make a fire under most any conditions. Creating a fire can make the difference between life and death in many outdoor survival situations, for this reason, it is a good skill to master.

Making a fire is extremely important for a number of reasons. Fire is important to keep flying insects and dangerous animals away. Cooking, purifying water, and bandage sterilization is possible with a fire. It is also a tool for signaling help in a survival situation out in the wilderness.

To make a fire, you must have three things: air, heat, and fuel. Without these three components, fire is not possible and the rate of survival, in many instances, is decreased.

First, begin making a fire by selecting the best location. It depends what you are planning to do with the fire, to determine the best location. Keep your fire near your shelter for convenience. Also, in signaling situations, you will want your fire to be highly visible. Choose the area wisely before you begin the process of making a fire.

A campfire must start with small pieces of wood and then progress to larger timbers. Avoid collecting wood directly from the earth because it is probably damp. Damp wood will not work well to start a fire. Your efforts will be futile.

To begin a fire, you will need tender. Tender is absolutely dry material that requires only a spark to ignite. Paper, if you have some available, will work well. Dry leaves, bark, and grass also make great tender to start a fire.

Once you get the fire started, progress from the tender to kindling. Kindling is dry sticks and twigs that are readily combustible. When placed on a small flame, kindling should start burning quickly and easily.

Once the fire has begun burning, you can begin adding larger pieces of wood to the area. The fire can continue to burn well with proper maintenance and attention.

Your outdoor survival kit should include items to start the fire such as tender, a candle, and waterproof matches. A flint striker is another method to make a fire. This method provides a spark that will get the flame to burn.

The finer and drier the tender, the easier it is to start the fire. Fluff the tender well to simplify the fire making process. If the outdoor survival kit doesn't have tender, use your knife to cut and chop dry sticks and bark to create tender. Remember the smaller the pieces the better. Place the flint striker at the tender and strike to create sparks. The sparks should make the tender catch fire. Sheltering the fire area from the wind when first making the sparks can be helpful.

Practice using these survival skills before an emergency to best be prepared. Making a fire is extremely important to survival. Learning the skill to making a fire will be extremely beneficial if you are ever placed in an outdoor survival situation.

How to Use a Compass for Survival

If you have a compass in your possession, you have what you need to determine your direction of travel. The trouble is, knowing how to use it. It is possible to learn how to use a compass alone for survival.

The red and white arrow on your compass is called the compass needle. The first thing you need to know, is that the red arrow is always pointing to the magnetic north pole of the earth. Don't confuse this with the black or white arrow on your compass. This is a common mistake.

If you want to travel north, you have it made. But, what if you want to travel in another direction? Now, what do you do with it?

The compass housing is the thing on the compass that turns. There is usually a scale on the edge of the compass housing. The scale typically goes from 0 to 360 or 0 to 400. These represent the degrees or the azimuth.

The letters N, E, S, and W, represent the directions North, East, South, and West, respectively. Let us assume that you want to travel northwest in the direction of the nearest town. What do you do next?

Locate northwest on the compass housing. Turn the housing until northwest is aligned with the large travel arrow on your compass.

Hold the compass flat in your hand so that the arrow can freely move. Now, turn your entire body, hand and compass until the compass needle is in line with the lines on the compass housing. Make certain the compass housing has not turned during this step. If the compass is not relatively flat, it will not be able to work effectively. This will throw off your direction.

Be careful you note the red arrow is pointing toward the north portion of the compass housing. If the south or white arrow is pointing in that direction, you will begin walking in the exact opposite direction of where you want to travel. This is a common mistake, so take the time to doublecheck for accuracy.

Once you have started walking in the desired direction, it is important to stay on track by checking your compass frequently. Do not continuously stare at the compass. Maybe choose an item off in the distance to aim for, then check the compass to make sure you are on course. For instance, you want to walk toward the tall tree or mountain
    the distance.

Walk toward help by being aware of the direction of a local town, highway, or river. Coupling your compass with a map can further assist you to finding your way, but when maps are not available, the compass can provide your life the direction it needs.

Your compass is a tool for survival. Learn how to use it properly before you need to use it to save your life. Practice using your compass in this method in areas that are familiar to you. This will give you a method for mastering this survival skill without the risk of danger by getting lost or disoriented.

Knives And Survival Knives

The knife has come to symbolize to the modern men the essence of survival and the ability to provide all that is needed for survival with one simple and lethal tool. A good knife is indeed better than most material things, it can provide protection and the ability to hunt and prepare food, it can also help in building a shelter and creating small objects that are vital for survival.

A few generations ago, maybe even less than a hundred years ago, men would not leave their house without a proper knife was only common sense to take a knife with you wherever you went, you never knew into what situations you run into, if you will get lost and will need to survive for a couple of days in the wild or if you will be surprised by some enemy or thief and will need to protect yourself.

For those of us who know knives it is a simple fact that no one knife can have all the features in it, every knife has its advantages and anyone using a knife will have to make his own decision as to what kind of things are important for him to have on his knife. It is not only the extra features of the knife that matter, it is also the way the knife itself is crafted and what it is made off.

Today most people are looking for a knife to serve them when they are away for a few days, or sometimes a few weeks, they need something that is very basic and that will provide them with the safety that it could potentially help them in case something goes wrong.

Not long ago I read in the paper that a diver had to use his knife to protect himself against a shark. The diver did not stab the shark as it was trying to attack him, but simply hit the shark on his nose with the blunt side of the knife did the job and the shark away though he use his knife as it was planned to be used, this diver had the right instinct, and he went for his knife.

In any case, when you are out camping, hiking, fishing or diving you will probably consider buying yourself a knife, and you should think about what you need before you even set foot in the shop. Try and think of the environments you are going to be in, and your needs, sometimes someone does need to hunt with his knife, but does not need to prepare the food from the hunted animal in some cases you will be walking through a jungle and you might want to use the knife to carve your way out of some thick bushes.

If you do your research and spend some time thinking of what you need you will have a better starting point and use the for information about different kinds of knives, I am sure you will be surprised from the wide verity of products out on the market.

Cold Weather Survival

Six hours from the trail head, 2 hours past his turn-around time and with storms filling in from the valley, Alex Theissen was at the edge of panic. What had started as a unremarkable spring outing in the White Mountains was going south quickly and the prospect of spending the night exposed at the timberline, with plummeting temperatures and not much more than some hard cheese and a foil survival blanket was becoming a distinct reality.

The impending sense of panic is familiar to any individual stranded on a windward shore with a gale coming on, disoriented in a maze of bike trails or caught, like Theissen on an exposed ridge with foul weather on the horizon. In many cases, what happens next is the crux moment wherein survival or full blown disaster ensues. In the case of Theissen, survival started with the acronym, S.T.O.P.

Sit ... Think ...Observe ... Plan ...

Rather than giving in to an all-too-human panic response, Theissen sat, took stock and acted in a way that likely saved his life. What follows is a briefing on what went through his head ... it's a lesson applicable to all hikers, hunters, canoeists and others who find themselves exposed and unprepared in falling or already frigid temperatures.

Shelter / Warmth

In cold temperatures, exposure can kill before anything else has a chance. In Theissen's case, staying above the timberline was untenable; thus getting below the was his first priority. After that he would need to find or create shelter, and finally (if possible) create warmth.

While it's beyond the scope of this article to describe shelter making or fire building in detail (shelter can be found in tree wells, in snow caves, and in the hollows of river banks; tinder is less available in winter than summer, none-the-less evergreens will often yield dry needles, pitch impregnated bark can often be sourced and if the snow-pack is not so deep as to disallow it, reserves of dry leaves and grass can be found under trees, rock overhangs and in tree wells), suffice it say that without either, chance of survival diminish.

What Theissen did was find a root cavity that provided both shelter and tinder; he sealed it as completely as possible with packed snow, and insulated himself from the ground using evergreen boughs. He managed to nurse a fire which, while it really never took, provided a certain degree of comfort and localized heat.

Route Finding

There was no way Theissen was going to find his way back to the trailhead in the impending whiteout. And it needs to be stressed; there was NO way he should have tried ... even descending to the was a challenge. That said, he was not lost and he had to keep it that way.

Route finding depends on visibility; thus traveling at night, in a whiteout or in heavily wooded terrain increases the chances of becoming lost. It's doubly important in these conditions to think, observe and plan ... and to acknowledge that it's not always prudent to act. It's often better to stay put than it is to flounder around in unfamiliar terrain risking further disorientation and injury.

By marking his return route to the ridgeline, and traveling only so far as required to ensure shelter, Theissen knew that once visibility returned he would be able to find his way back to the trailhead.

Creating Visibility

If all went well, Theissen would hole up for the night in his makeshift shelter and walk out the following morning. This presumes of course, that he wasn't lost. If he were, creating the conditions to be found would be his next priority. Experts agree that the three following elements will increase the chances of a rescue party locating a lost hiker...

Visibility - created by smudge fires, markers, signals

Positioning - on ridgelines, open riverbanks, at the
    Mobility (or lack thereof) - stationary targets are easier to find

Had Theissen been lost, he would have returned to the ridgeline when conditions allowed, created visibility (stamped a signal in the snow,

anchored his foil blanket, built a smudge fire ...) and not strayed from
the area.

Hydration

It hardly needs said, that if you've got fuel and a means to light it, the
ice and snow you're surrounded with are a viable source of hydration. If
not, there are other sources. Depending on how cold it is, flowing water
is frequently available under the snow pack in the bottom of creeks
and at river bends. Animals and birds will keep patches of swamps and
ponds ice-free. In the alpine, solar radiation can be powerful enough
to create ice-melt against dark rock faces.

Nutrition

Nutrition can be more difficult, and needs to figure heavily in any self-
rescue plan. Cold weather requires more calories from the body and,
while it is possible to live weeks without food, hunger is debilitating
and lowers the resistance to cold and the ability to cope.

There is good reason why survival literature frequently describes frozen
landscapes as arid ... there's not much alive, and there's not much to
eat. As flippant as it seems to say it: getting out sooner than later
is a very good idea. Once the situation has stabilized all efforts need
to turn towards positioning one's self to being found or logically and
methodically finding one's way out. One dies of starvation sooner in
winter than summer.

As it turns out, the Theissen's storm passed and by 3am the were lit by
a brilliant moon. There was enough light for Theissen to return to the
ridge line and find the marked descent by dawn. The previous day he had
stupidly decided to ignore his turn-around time. Every decision after
that however was the right one, and by early afternoon the following
day he was back at his car hungry tired and sheepish ... but alive.

Natural Health Remedies for Insect Bites and Stings

Almost anywhere you reside on this planet there are small creatures, tiny insects that attack to sting or bite you, either because they see you as a threat to their very existence or as food for their survival.

Insect bite appearance is noticeable by one or more red bumps which are extremely itchy. Yes, you want to scratch it - but don't! Easier said than done I know; problem is, scratching will exacerbate the itchiness and make it bleed.

If you have a tick, flee or a mosquito bite, they have been feeding off you; and most irksome is the thought of that nasty itchy bump left behind from a mosquito is actually full of its saliva.

Insect stings are commonly ants, bees and wasps; their sting penetrates your skin injecting poison into you.

Whilst ants and wasps will sting you several times, a bee stings once, leaving its stinger under your skin with a sac full of venom on the surface. The tendency is to panic and try to brush it off with your hand; this only serves to pump in more of the venom as will trying to remove it with your fingertips or tweezers.

Yes, it's a bit of a shock and it hurts! Keep a cool head, slide your fingernail under the sac and scrape away the sting. You could use the edge of a, not too sharp knife, or the edge of your bank or credit card.

A bee sting or a wasp sting can cause an allergic reaction which could be fatal if not treated urgently - medical attention is required immediately!

The symptoms of allergic reaction, called anaphylaxis, are: hives, swelling in the mouth and/or throat, laboured breathing and rapid heart rate.

If you have many bites and stings, and you don't have an allergic reaction you are not out of danger - you must seek medical attention immediately!

We'll assume you have been stung once - the bee sting is out - with no reaction.

Here are some natural health solutions to treat insect stings:

. For a bee sting, stir a teaspoon of bicarbonate of soda in a glass of water until dissolved; then use a cotton wool bud to dip into the solution wetting the area, and then place it directly on the sting securing it with sticky tape.

. For a wasp sting, dip the cotton wool bud into vinegar; as with a bee sting, wet the area first, and then place it directly on the sting securing it with sticky tape.

. If you have Papaya handy, place a slice on the sting area. Papaya has enzymes that bring down inflammation and swelling.

. Garlic or onion rubbed on the sting site will do the job as well.

. Crush an aspirin, adding to water making a paste, apply to the sting to reduce the swelling. (WARNING: if you have an aspirin allergy DO NOT apply aspirin ever! And DO NOT use aspirin to treat children).

. Applying sugar works just as well to bring down the swelling

. Try rubbing on Calendula cream to reduce itching or a few drops of Lavender oil or Tea tree oil.

If you take a walks through forests, woodlands, meadows or moors, be aware that ticks attach to your skin; and as the little vampire tick bites and feeds off your blood they may infect you with Lyme disease, a bacteria called 'Borrelia burgdorferi' which must be treated by a doctor.

If you find a tick on your body, use tweezers as close to the skin as you can, gently pull until it free; try not to break the head or it will stay latched to your skin and cause infection.

Once the tick is free, apply an antiseptic.

What to do about those mosquito bites, flee bites and other biting insects:

. Don't scratch

. Applying an ice cube to the bite will reduce itching

. Bites can be treated with essential oils. Apply a few drops of eucalyptus oil, clove oil or peppermint oil on a cotton wool bud

. Roll-on or spray deodorants are known to work - give it a try

. Check your toothpaste label; if it has peppermint smear it on the bite

How do you prevent these pesky parasite's bites and stings?

Eat a couple of cloves of garlic daily before and when you go outside. Your sweat glands release the garlic smell repelling most insects.

Don't like garlic?

You can use a repellent called Permethrin, a natural insecticidal property originally found in chrysanthemums. Permethrin is now sold in a spray can as a synthesized man-made insecticide.

Spray it on the clothes you plan to go out in and hang them to dry. Make sure they are not light, bright coloured clothes as they will only attract the little varmints!

Mosquito Bites Treatment

Whatever corner the globe you are domiciled, there will always be pestering minute creatures you will find such a total disturbance. It is said that there are more species of their kind than all the others placed all together. They are identified to be very successful in their means of survival because they can easily adopt to whatever sort of environment.

Even if they are considered as the smallest that ever existed on , they bring a lot of hazards. Over the years, there have already been plenty of casualties due to their attacks. One of those that should be given much attention to are mosquito bites treatment.

Mosquito bites treatment is such an important issue especially to those who are living in tropical regions because if not looked into with high regard, it can be very lethal. Malaria Fever, Dog Heart Worm, Yellow Fever, West Nile Virus, Dengue Fever and Systemic Lupus Erythematosus are just among the fatal diseases that can unmistakably lead to death. They will always be feeding themselves through humans albeit, there are some that also do with animals, because they are parasitic.

It means that they live off a host rather than devouring it. They are experts in the field of preying other existing classes that thrive. An example is that they suck out blood in order for them to complete the process of reproduction.

The latest type of antihistamines and anaesthetics can bring temporary yet quick mosquito bites treatment. the other hand, hydrocortisone cream may have a slower relief but has longer effect. Even just a single percent of its application can improve the condition. Two percent of Xylocaine Gel can result in immediate respite from surface itching. Such is the main symptom people do just to control the skin assault. As for those are experiencing edema and aches, Ibuprofen Gel is a perfect remedy for stings.

As for other cited grave conditions, it should be readily seen by a physician to diagnose the proper mosquito bites treatment. It can include rashes wherever they will occur, shortness of breath, swelling in the face, light- headedness or difficulty in swallowing. All of those mentioned can take place within minutes or to an hour after the tingle brought by the insect.

When it comes to local reactions, it does not really require professional care. Although, it is not a reason to be lax because there have been instances it only worsened in the following days. If it keeps on distracting you from performing normal activities, it is recommended you go to the nearest doctor for check-up. For home medications, baking soda and meat can destroy venoms based on protein. There may none ample scientific explanations to back it up but it makes rational sense.

Wilderness Survival: What To Do When Things Don't Go As You Planned

Being in the great outdoors enjoying nature is a great way to spend your free time. The wilderness is very exciting, but it can also be very dangerous when things don't go as you planned. The very best action plan is to always be prepared for such a scenario to take place. You never know when you may get lost, injured, or have to stay longer than planned due to the weather. Keep children close to you at all times so they don't get lost or attacked by animals.

Even if you plan to only be in the wilderness for a short period of time make sure others know where you went and when you should arrive back. This way if you don't return they know where to start rescue efforts and when. Always dress in layers so that you can add or remove clothing as needed. It can get very hot or very cool in just a few hours out there so be ready for it.

You should always carry a survival pack with necessities. Your supplies should include plenty of water or water purification tablets, dry food, a first aid kit, a cell phone, emergency flares, and a flashlight. It is very important that you stay hydrated and alert if you become lost in the wilderness. If you are with other people make sure everyone stays together and talk yourselves through the situation. Make sure you secure a safe place to sleep should it appear you may be there throughout the night.

The wilderness is a great place to explore and get back to nature. It offers a relaxing break from our hectic lives. However, people do get lost in the wilderness and things always go according to plan. By always being prepared for such an event, you have the very best chance of remaining calm and having your basic needs met until help arrives.

Easy Survival Skills

1. Put dried moss or milkweed fuzz in your pocket as you walk, so you'll have dry tinder to start a fire, just in case it's raining later. Cattail fuzz works well too, and you can experiment with different materials.

2. If it looks and tastes like a blueberry, strawberry, or raspberry - it is. There is no berry in North America that looks like a blueberry, strawberry, or raspberry, and can hurt you from one taste. Take a taste, and just spit it out completely if it doesn't taste right.

3. Make a pile of dry leaves and dead grass to keep warm in an emergency. I have slept warmly without a blanket, in below-freezing weather, in a pile of dry grass.

4. Put a stick upright in the ground, and mark the tip of the shadow. Mark it again fifteen minutes later. Scratch a line between the first and second marks, and it will be pointing east. Techniques like this can save you when your compass is lost.

5. Clouds form in the Rocky Mountains just before the afternoon storms in summer. Hikers are regularly killed by lightning in Colorado. Birds often fly lower before storms. Learning to read the sky and the behavior of animals can keep you out of trouble.

6. The biggest wilderness killer is hypothermia, and getting wet is the biggest cause. Get in the habit of watching for ledges or large fir trees to stand under when you think rain may be coming. Learning to stay

dry is one of the more important survival skills.

7. To stay warmer, sleep with your head slightly downhill. It takes some getting used to, but it works.

8. Get in the habit of filling water bottles every chance you get, and you won't have such a hard time with any long dry stretches of trail. Drink up the last of your water right before you fill the bottles too.

9. Break a "blister" on the trunk of a small spruce or fir tree, and you can use the sap that oozes out as an good antiseptic dressing for small cuts. It also can be used to start a fire, and will burn when wet.

10. Bark from a white birch tree will usually light even when wet. In a jam, you can also use it as a paper substitute if you need to leave a note in an emergency.

You now have the knowledge to increase your chances of surviving unforeseen situations and always remember to prepare for the worst but hope for the best.